IMAGES

of America

RICHMOND

Edward Saunders, Janet House, and Gertrude Edmonds appeared in Hazel Crandall's elaborate Mother Goose recital in 1939. Carolina Free Baptist Church can be seen in the background.

On the cover: Richmond Lace Works was clearly a busy place! (Courtesy of the Richmond Historical Society.)

IMAGES
of America

RICHMOND

Kirk W. House

ARCADIA
PUBLISHING

Published by Arcadia Publishing
Charleston SC, Chicago IL, Portsmouth NH, San Francisco CA

Library of Congress Catalog Card Number: 2006940477

For all general information contact Arcadia Publishing at:
Telephone 843-853-2070
Fax 843-853-0044
E-mail sales@arcadiapublishing.com
For customer service and orders:
Toll-Free 1-888-313-2665

Visit us on the Internet at www.arcadiapublishing.com

Dedicated with thanks to those long-term dwellers in Richmond,
my grandparents, my aunts, and my uncles:
Roland C. Dow and Doris Kenyon Dow
Janice Dow Baton and Erlo Baton
Harold House and Ethel Donellan House
Eleanor House Smith and Earl Smith
Janet House King and Alan King

CONTENTS

ACKNOWLEDGMENTS

This book would not have been possible without the collection of the Richmond Historical Society, held at the Clark Memorial Library in Carolina. I owe a debt of thanks to Patricia Smith Millar, who introduced me to the collection and helped me through it, and to the library staff, who cheerfully welcomed me during bleary-eyed days of scouring and scanning. Both institutions are jewels of the community, and anyone at all interested in the town's heritage should take out an annual membership in the Richmond Historical Society. My son Joshua B. House, who so often contributes to the preparation of my books, helped me with the original review of images and with some jaunts around town.

All undesignated photographs come from the historical society collection. Others are marked as being from the collections of Langworthy Public Library in Hope Valley (LPL), Harold B. House (HBH), Deborah A. House (DAH), or the author. Thanks very much to all those who shared.

Those looking for more details on Richmond history might try *Driftways Into the Past*, published by the Richmond Historical Society; *Water Power Revisited: A Circle of Dam Sites on the Wood and Pawcatuck Rivers*, by Gladys Segar and Betty Salomon; and *The Story of a Mill Village: Carolina, Rhode Island*, by Vera Main Robinson. They are all well worth the study!

With water power vital to industry for some 200 years, many communities in Richmond and neighboring towns grew up on stream banks. Since Wood River and the Pawcatuck River form the western and southern boundaries of Richmond, some of those villages—like Carolina, Alton, Hope Valley, and Wyoming, among others—spill into other towns. So does this book, from time to time.

INTRODUCTION

My first memories are of growing up in what once had been a mill duplex on Main Street (Route 138) in the Richmond village of Wyoming. They were good memories, and I found it a good place to live. So have many others through three centuries and more. Some of my family was in town by 1700 or so, and many are still there now.

Like its sister towns in rural Rhode Island, Richmond (part of Charlestown from 1738 to 1747, and even earlier part of Westerly) has no lesser administrative divisions, and no central metropolis. The villages are as unofficial as they are fascinating, and many homes lie in the long stretches between settlements.

Keeping track of those villages can challenge the newcomer, or even the old-timer. For instance Alton has also been known as Alton Plains, Plainville, or even just The Plains, while Wyoming was once called Alton—after starting life as Brand's Iron Works. Hillsdale is hard to find these days, although Hillsdale Road still runs, as it always did, past the Devil's Punchbowl and No Bottom Pond.

For a lightly-populated rural town, Richmond was also an incubator of early American industry. There are about 31 dam sites in Richmond, and water released through most of those dams powered millstones, lumber saws, and, of course, textile looms. Some of these plants still operate, just as farms still dot the landscape. But golf courses seem to be a rising land use, while Wyoming has become a retail center and Wood River Junction is home to several Chariho schools.

Like much of New England, Richmond in a single lifetime has watched the transition from pheasants (an introduced old-world game bird) back to the native wild turkey, who has paced the forest's resurgence as more and more land has gone out of cultivation. Even the otter and the beaver are back. Trekkers in the woods are sometime puzzled by cellar holes with no sign of their old foundations, but the riddle is simply answered—when the state paved Route 138, the farmers hauled out their old stone and sold it to be crushed for gravel.

Even as some parts of town have become wilder, others are tamer now. I well remember hiking with my dad along the stony Smallpox Trail, now a very nice road with very fine homes. While many Richmonders now drive to work elsewhere, others still earn their bread on the farm, in the mill, at the teacher's desk, or behind the shop counter, just as our ancestors did long ago. You will met some of those ancestors in the pages of this book, and I hope you like them. It's been a joy and a privilege to bring them to you.

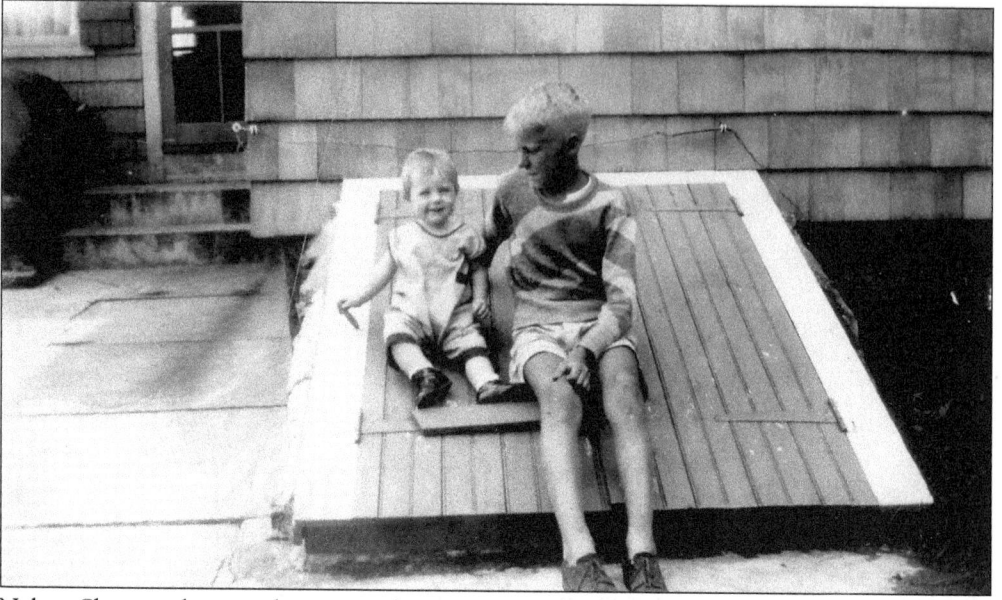

Nelson Sherman keeps a close eye on his cousin Carolyn Dow. (Courtesy of HBH.)

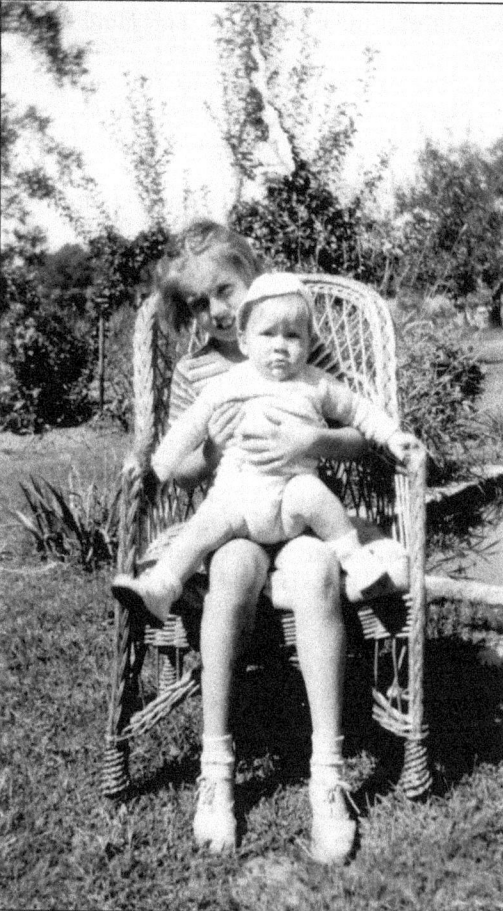

Janice Dow looks after Bobby Boss.
(Courtesy of DAH.)

One

PEOPLE POWER

Poultry farming is an old tradition in Richmond, although most growers go to the chickens, rather than having the chickens come to them. (Courtesy of DAH.)

Rita Boss, Doris Dow, and Ruth Nimmo took a turn outside in Wyoming on Thanksgiving Day of 1943. Droopy stockings indicate that despite wartime shortages of silk and nylon, the black market was alive and well. Just visible in the right background is the large Dr. Frederick Edwards home, now the site of a filling station. (Courtesy of HBH.)

143|105

AR UNITED STATES OF AMERICA
OFFICE OF PRICE ADMINISTRATION

WAR RATION BOOK TWO

IDENTIFICATION

Omar E. Barber
(Name of person to whom book is issued)

Main
(Street number or rural route)

Carolina ___ *Rhode Island* ___ *77* *M* *143105*
(City or post office) (State) (Age) (Sex)

ISSUED BY LOCAL BOARD NO. *155.6* *Washington* *R.I.*
(County)

Wyoming ___ *Richmond*
(Street address of local board) (City) (State)

By _____ *Jeanne C. Lees*
(Signature of issuing officer)

SIGNATURE _____ *Omar E. Barber*

(To be signed by the person to whom this book is issued. If such person is unable to sign because of age or incapacity, another may sign in his behalf)

WARNING

1 This book is the property of the United States Government. It is unlawful to sell or give it to any other person or to use it or permit anyone else to use it, except to obtain rationed goods for the person to whom it was issued.
2 This book must be returned to the War Price and Rationing Board which issued it, if the person to whom it was issued is inducted into the armed services of the United States, or leaves the country for more than 30 days, or dies. The address of the Board appears above.
3 A person who finds a lost War Ration Book must return it to the War Price and Rationing Board which issued it.
4 PERSONS WHO VIOLATE RATIONING REGULATIONS ARE SUBJECT TO $10,000 FINE OR IMPRISONMENT, OR BOTH.

OPA Form No. R-121   16—30858-1

During World War II all residents from infants on up had their ration books, and local officials had to manage them.

A World War II aircraft-spotting tower stood in Hope Valley, in the field between Spring Street and Soap House Lane. Zenith Wright Sherman and Doris Kenyon Dow took their turns defending Hope Valley and Wyoming from the Luftwaffe. Dow is sticking her tongue out at them. (Courtesy of DAH.)

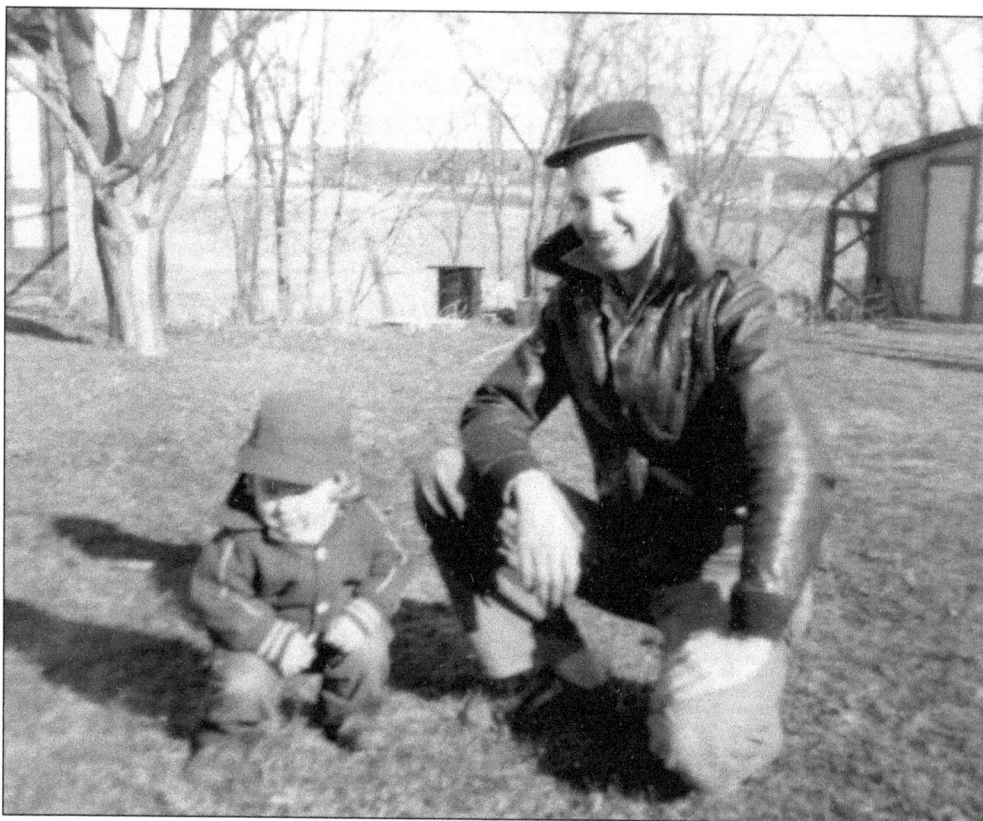

Ten years later, the World War II flight jacket gets more down-to-earth usage. (Courtesy of HBH.)

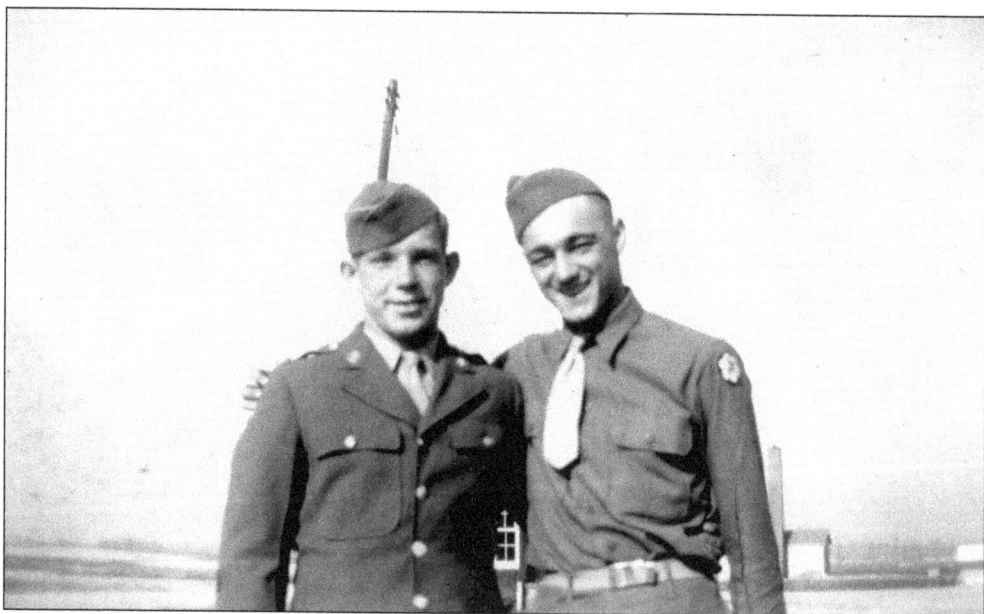

Dozens of Richmonders, and many more from neighboring towns, served in the war. (Courtesy of DAH.)

Adam Cekala married Marjorie Dow in a wartime ceremony. (Courtesy of DAH.)

Nelson Sherman became a sergeant in the U.S. Army. (Courtesy of DAH.)

Harold B. House served in the Army Air Forces. (Courtesy of HBH.)

Sixteen-year-old Marcus Whitford left Tug Hollow to join the navy in 1916, a year ahead of the United States' entry into the First World War. Recalled to duty in World War II, he commanded a division of mine sweepers (as well as individual vessels, some of whose construction he supervised). Whitford participated in the actions at Makin and Okinawa, and served as chairman of the Judge Advocate General's Review Board in the postwar period. He received the first Rhode Island Star in 1957. On Memorial Day 1986, Louise Burton congratulated Capt. Marcus Whitford, USN-Ret., on his being awarded the Rhode Island Cross.

Richmond's militia served in the Revolutionary War, and Richmonders joined up for most, if not all, of America's conflicts. David R. Kenyon (First Rhode Island) was wounded at Fredericksburg in 1862, and made captain before being mustered out a few months later. He named his first son Charles Lincoln Kenyon, indicating that he was still an enthusiastic Unionist even after disaster at Fredericksburg.

Col. John Stanton Slocum was wounded at the First Battle of Bull Run, and died two days later.

BATTLE FLAG
3D RHODE ISLAND HEAVY ARTILLERY

Many stars have been snipped from the battle flag of the 3rd Rhode Island Heavy Artillery, possibly as souvenirs for surviving veterans.

James Johnson was quite the dude in a bygone day.

The Chester Sherman home fills the background in this photograph of Doris Kenyon Dow, who always felt that she could have made her life on the stage. (Courtesy of HBH.)

An old Hillsdale clan, cheerfully gathered for a wedding, from left to right includes Harold B. House, Carolyn Dow House, Jordy King, Debby King, Eleanor House Smith, Patricia Smith Millar, and Janet House King. (Courtesy of HBH.)

These bridesmaids (from left to right, Helen Dow, Janice Dow, Monya Nadolny Bryant, Katherine Cekala, and unidentified) are celebrating the Adam Cekala-Marjorie Dow wedding at the new St. Joseph's church in 1943. (Courtesy of DAH.)

One couple in this earlier wedding party is unidentified, but Patricia Smith and Raymond Gardiner are looking on while Peggy Wheeler and Lowell Hawkins tie the knot. Robert Parker is enthusiastically officiating.

Eleanor House Smith was an active participant in the Grange and in the Richmond Historical Society. (Courtesy of HBH.)

This family group seems excessively glum for a nice summer day. Notice the little girl's doll.

This early church crowd, congregation and edifice both uncertain, also seems particularly solemn.

The women's group at Wood River Church, on the other hand, looks as though it is ready to have a good time.

This Wood River Sunday school picnic is reaching all ages.

Pastor Clifford Bond (center) and church president Paul DeGannett (left) are in front of the old Wood River Church in 1972. Bond simultaneously pastored Seventh-Day Baptist churches in Hopkinton. DeGannett was clerk of the works when Richmond School was built. (Author's collection.)

Addie May Chase cut quite a figure in the style of an earlier day. She lived from 1876 to 1943.

Estelle F. Kenyon Sheldon, wife of John C. Sheldon, likewise sported the requisite ladies' headgear.

Dr. Ed Kenyon (far left) and his wife Ida May (far right) pose with their grandchildren in 1915. Dr. Kenyon's nurse joins them, third from left.

Florence G. Hoxsie and friends took a little bicycle outing to Alton. From left to right are (first row) Katie May Bresford Crandall, Kate Barber, and Eva McInnes; (second row) Emma Babcock and Hoxsie.

Rev. Daniel Davis, born a Maryland slave in 1834, escaped at age 26 and came to Carolina for schooling in 1865. He married Almira Esther Brundage (or Bundy) and lived and preached in Alton until his death in the early 20th century. The Town of Richmond contributed to his monument.

Almost alone for many years, Princess Redwing urged the recovery of Narragansett and Wampanoag identity. Redwing, a maternal relative of Alton's Ellison "Tarzan" Brown, was with Brown when he scored his first Boston Marathon victory in 1936.

Lucy Irene Gammell and Roy Wilson Rawlings toured the country in 1909, appearing in the centennial production *Lincoln in the White House*. (Courtesy of LPL.)

Settling down in Richmond, the young Rawlings couple started a family. (Courtesy of LPL.)

Lucy "Kate" Rawlings felt great affection for the "ancient home" of the Thomas Lillibridge family. "Out of respect for what it stood for in this America of ours, I planted old fashioned flowers to cover the scars of time." (Courtesy of LPL.)

Roy Rawlings would have a lengthy career in the state House of Representatives. (Courtesy of LPL.)

Lucy (the younger) and Rob Roy Rawlings pose with their mother in this 1924 image. Both children would follow their father into the general assembly. Lucy Rawlings Tootel would go to the House of Representatives for Richmond, Charlestown, and Hopkinton, campaigning with such slogans as "We Love Lucy" and "Lucy Rides Again." (Courtesy of LPL.)

Rob Roy would serve in the state senate, representing Richmond and its neighboring South County towns. (Courtesy of LPL.)

Support from disgruntled Democrats helped make Republican Roy Rawlings speaker of the house (in Providence). This image is from 1931. (Courtesy of LPL.)

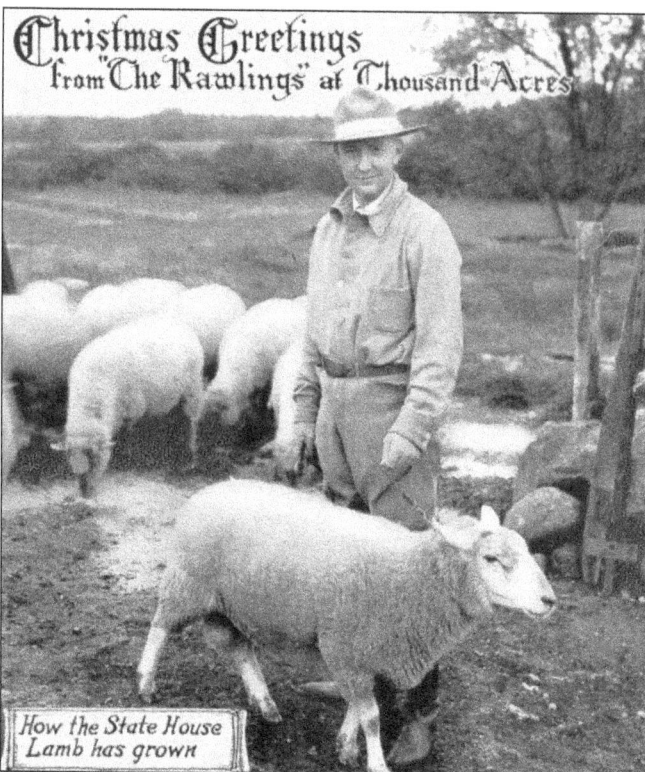

Christmas Greetings from "The Rawlings" at Thousand Acres

How the State House Lamb has grown

Legislators got $5 a day back then, for a maximum of 60 days. Corn and sheep kept the Rawlings clan going.

Speaker Roy Rawlings and state attorney general Charles P. Sisson seem quite cheerful in each other's company in this 1927 photograph, but they had earlier clashed when Rawlings pressed the appointment of a woman doctor as medical examiner in Richmond. Sisson ruled that a woman could be named, then suddenly reversed himself. In the end, with notable sound and fury, the appointment went through as Rawlings wanted. (Courtesy of LPL.)

DON'T BLOT OUT RICHMOND ON FEB. 28

THE State of Rhode Island, thru Republican Legislation, spends annually in Richmond: For schools $8,000.00; for roads $104,500.00; for policing $8,000.00; for agriculture $1,000.00 - a total of $121,500.00.

Democratic Bills Senate 51, 121, 27, 7 and House 721, 884, 512 and many others propose to take away, not only these aids from the Town, but Richmond's representation and vote in the Senate itself.

A Republican Vote on February 28 Will Help Guarantee These Benefits.

VOTE FOR THE REPUBLICAN CANDIDATE ➤➤

Frederick W. Smith

For many years Fred Smith operated an automobile and farm equipment dealership across from Richmond Town Hall, with another in Wakefield.

DEC. 31, 1915

Richmond, R. I.,   790

Received of H. Fred Clark -

One   Dollars,

Poll
it being for Town Tax assessed September, 1905.

Poll Tax, $ 1.00

Interest,

$ 1.00

BRADFORD B. MOORE,
COLLECTOR OF TAXES,
RICHMOND, R. I.

Chas. Greene
Town Treas.   Collector.

Tax collection, of course, is always a necessity.

Hazel Dyson was a long-serving town clerk.

In the 1930s, Byron "Beanie" Smith, like many local residents, hunted for food more than sport. The family farm was on the west side of Hillsdale Road, just south of Hoxie Road.

Two

Town Around

Carolina, which at one time had its own library, is one of a dozen or more villages and settlements that dot the forests and fields of Richmond. Like many riverside communities, Carolina spills into the neighboring municipality—in this case, Charlestown.

Richmond is now served by Clark Memorial Library in Carolina (originally in Shannock). Upstairs space holds the Richmond Historical Society collections. The name honors four Clarks killed in the 1938 hurricane.

Carolina F. B. Church,

Rev. S. Miller

Carolina Free Baptist Church is still an important part of life in that village.

The Washington County
Pomona Grange Fair grew from
a small get-together to the
largest fair in Rhode Island,
with a permanent home off
Route 112 in Richmond. It
is an eagerly-awaited event,
drawing visitors from across
southern New England.

WASHINGTON COUNTY

FAIR

AUGUST 16 — 20

FREE PARKING

Children under 12
FREE

GIGANTIC MIDWAY

PROGRAM

Fishing remains an important part of life in Richmond.

New laws and deeper knowledge now prohibit the shooting of hawks.

The mill village of Shannock, also home to a New Haven Railroad depot, owed its original existence to this dam on the Pawcatuck River. Long ago the Narragansetts defeated the Pequots in a battle for fishing rights at the falls here.

Shannock has recently been undergoing a process of gentrification. This Main Street view will be familiar to older residents.

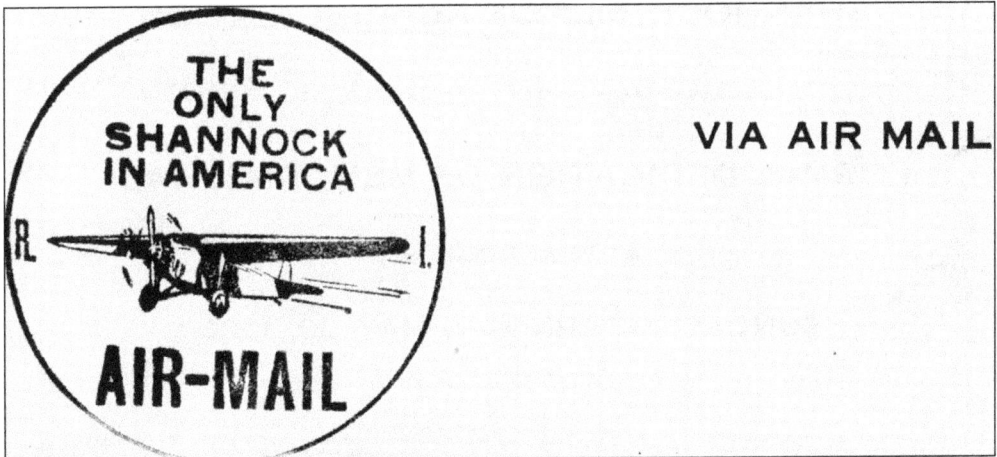

THE ONLY SHANNOCK IN AMERICA

R. I.

AIR-MAIL

VIA AIR MAIL

Being the only Shannock in America is an occasion of pride. The name comes from the Narragansett word for squirrel.

Shannock Memorial Hall for many years was a center of community life.

SHANNOCK MEMORIAL ASSOCIATION

ESPECIALLY INVITES YOU TO ATTEND THE

FORMAL DEDICATION OF MEMORIAL HALL

AT SHANNOCK, R. I.

SUNDAY AFTERNOON, MAY 30, 1920

AT 3 O'CLOCK

The hall's dedication was a well-justified occasion of community pride.

The Thayer barn, outside Shannock, presents a lovely view, yet common in still-rural Richmond.

This map for the Johnny Cake Festival gives a feel for the tiny but beautiful village of Usquepaugh.

This farmhouse near Richmond's center was variously owned by Nelson K. Church, Janetta Brown, and Henry Kenyon.

Wood River Church

Records for Wood River Baptist Church go back to 1723, but the church is mentioned in the Shannock Purchase deed of 1709. Either date probably puts the congregation among the oldest half-dozen Baptist churches in America. This facility, built in the 1820s, now belongs to the cemetery association.

The current Wood River Church facility stands on Route 138 west of Richmond School. (Author's collection.)

Richmond Town House (across from the school) has been considerably enlarged since this photograph was taken. The monument in front honors disabled American veterans.

Wyoming Post Office, until about 1960, was in the house on the right, which still stands on Route 3. Just to the left is the Wood River Church Mission Rooms. Out of sight behind the Mission Rooms was the bridewell, or jail.

From left to right in this Wyoming view are the Oyster Saloon, Mary Bliven cottage, Bill Johnson house, Walter Kenyon house, Honorable Daniel Kinyon blacksmith shop, Honorable Daniel Kinyon cottage, and Honorable John C. Kinyon house. Readers can still see most of these structures, looking downhill from the Wyoming traffic light toward the bridge into Hopkinton. The gentlemen standing from left to right (not a habit to cultivate in today's traffic) are Peter Tarbox, Collins Cory, Joseph Colbert, George Davis, Stanton Barber, Herbert Watson, John Fuller, and Edward Barber.

From left to right in Wyoming (facing the opposite direction from the previous image) are the Dawley Tavern, the livery stable, the bank, and the Segar Store.

Many local homes employed granite in their fencing and foundations. The Parker House in Wyoming, seen here, employs granite in its fencing.

Wyoming Mill burned in 1903.

The Gates place, in old school district No. 8 (Tefft's Hill), shows shingle finish, fieldstone wall, central chimney, and barns—frequent features in local architecture.

The back of the Gates place shows other common features: the pump house, the wind lock/mudroom at the back door, and the saltbox roof. The house could be expanded simply by extending the front roofline down and building under it.

The white house at the left is the old Smith house, birthplace of Marcus Whitford. Next is the Reynolds Mill. The large willow tree for a time lent the name Willow Valley to this neighborhood, but the older name of Tug Hollow endured, possibly because the carriage shop (on the right) made tugs, or traces. Thomas W. Segar took this photograph.

It's Christmas Eve at "Thousand Acres" and Here's a toast to you!   The Rawlings

The Rawlings place lay along Meadow Brook.

First Baptist Church in Arcadia is now a private home.

Wood River, here running near Arcadia, forms most of the boundary between Richmond and Hopkinton.

Arcadia Pond, now more attractively wooded, is the site of a popular state park.

The Collins Store, near Wood River Junction, was also the post office.

Notice the old-fashioned railroad crossing markers in Wood River Junction, which is, by the way, traditionally the coldest spot in Rhode Island.

Mill tenements like these in Alton could be found throughout the region.

This view of Alton's Main Street includes the pre-1870 Wood River Chapel.

Wood River flows over the dam and under the bridge in Alton. Besides the swimmers perched at left, note the cyclist and the small boy up above.

This February 1891 photograph of the Jesse Crandall house in Hope Valley was shot by moonlight between 9:00 p.m. and 10:00 p.m. Reflection from the snow, and a long exposure, doubtless helped.

Three

WORK DAYS

Harold B. House, at around the age of 10 in this c. 1935 photograph, worked a team of horses at his father's farm on Hillsdale Road. Borrowed or rented from Duncan "Dunc" Wheeler in Beaver River, the horses were used, among other things, to relocate henhouses, which rested on sledge runners. Those houses blew away or apart in the 1938 hurricane, littering the landscape with dead chickens. (Courtesy of HBH.)

AUCTION!

WILL BE SOLD AT PUBLIC AUCTION
at the residence of Joseph C. Kenyon, Richmond Switch, at 10 o'clock A. M., THURSDAY

March 21, 1867,

(IF FAIR. IF NOT. THE NEXT FAIR WEEK DAY.)

The following articles, consisting of household furniture, &c., viz: one Bureau, two Bedsteads, one set of Chairs, two Rocking chairs, one Table, one Clock, one set of white Dishes, one parlor Stove, about sixty yds of Carpeting, nearly new, one Rooster and six Hens, one Iron bar, one grain Cradle, two Pitchforks, one covered Carraige, one silver trimmed Harness, one Fat Hog and other articles too numerous to mention.

JOSEPH C. KENYON.

☞ Conditions made known at time and place of Sale.

JOHN F. BAGGS,
Richmond, Mar. 11, 1867.]   Auctioneer.

Joseph C. Kenyon was one of a numerous clan, descended from two brothers and a cousin who immigrated from Lancashire, England, to South County by 1683.

This double home in the Carolina mill yard would have housed families of two managers or skilled workers. From left to right are Mrs. Brooks, Charlie Brooks, Walter Brooks, and George H. Goodhue.

The 1800s may have been the age of steam, but it was also still the age of the horse.

Dr. Milton Duckworth of Carolina obviously enjoyed both his dog Sport and his new Cadillac.

At one stage in his career, Duckworth used a more pedestrian vehicle. Notice that the lantern ahead of the left door has an upright equi-armed cross, no doubt with a red lens to identify him as he sped to emergency calls.

The crossing tender in Shannock had to clear the way across the tracks.

Mica was once a significant product, both in Shannock and in Wyoming.

The mill in the background still grinds Kenyon's Johnny Cake Meal on the banks of Queens River (Usquepaugh River, below the falls).

KENYON'S
Stone Ground
JOHNNY CAKE

WHITE
CORN MEAL

No additives - No preservatives

16 oz. (1 lb.) NET WT. 454 gr.

The general assembly once debated whether proper johnnycakes are made with hot milk (the Newport way) or boiling water (the South County way). South County cooks have been known to sneak in milk if the mixture gets too dry. One imaginative impresario now experiments with liquids as exotic as champagne or ginger ale, with excellent results. (Courtesy Kenyon Corn Meal Company.)

Roy Rawlings's place—now the Meadow Brook Golf Course—raised corn for johnnycake meal.

The Richmond Town Pound is justly famed for its impressive granite gateway pillars. The pound keeper, usually a nearby farmer, rounded up stray stock and penned them here until their owners arrived to drive or haul them off.

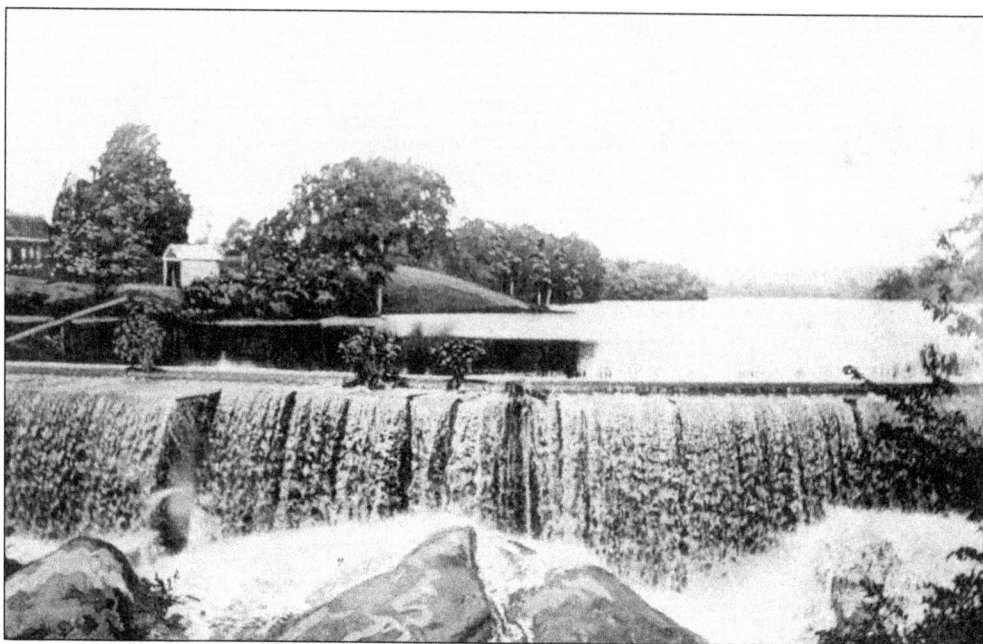

Wyoming Dam impounds Wyoming Pond on Wood River, creating a powerful head of water to be harnessed.

The mill and falls at Wyoming served numerous operations, in numerous structures, beginning before the Revolution and running past World War II.

Wyoming Mills, which later burned, occupied this site. Notice the curious tower, with sections variously canted.

In the time of this picture, the site was Fenner, Sheldon, and Tyler Batting and Ways Manufacturing Company. Later American Mica Company had the site, and mica still sparkles in the sandy lot. Notice the women workers on the right.

Dow Woolen Works was an extensive operation.

Part of the Dow Woolen Works stood on the Hopkinton side of Wyoming Dam.

A spectacular fire in the late 1940s put an end to most of Wyoming's mill work. The Dawley Tavern/Stagecoach House is seen just behind the chimney.

The mills are gone but enough of the dams and races remain to enthrall the student of industrial history. (Author's collection.)

Quite a crowd gathered around 1903 to watch state road workers on the job. Cutting down the hill that rose near the current junction of Route 3 and Route 138 was one of the first state jobs in Richmond, calling for men, boys, and horses. The long white building at right, once the Segar store, is now Boucher's Wood River Inn. Note that the road crew is racially mixed.

The Segar store, shown here, would be a Pioneer Store 50 years later.

Firefighters beat back a blaze at the Railroad Avenue underpass in Shannock.

Samuel Reynolds built this saltbox home, later moved by 40 pairs of oxen to a commanding position on the freshly-built New London Turnpike. There it became the Tug Hollow Gatehouse, collecting tolls and serving as a hostelry. A spectacular stabbing took place here one night around 1833.

The Tug Hollow Mill went up around 1810. It was at one time the Reynolds-Sheldon Carding Mill, while at another season Charles Lincoln Kenyon made baskets there. According to legend, Robert Reynolds counterfeited coins on the side. Both line drawings came from a feature in the 1898 *Providence Sunday Telegram*.

Notice the wooden fence, the dam, and the barn in this view of Tug Hollow Mill.

The stone-and-earth dam on Beaver River in Tug Hollow is typical of many throughout the area. Even streams seemingly insignificant powered Rhode Island industry for two centuries.

Even a short fall builds up a powerful head.

The street ran right through the Browning Mill in Arcadia.

Like other Richmond villages, Arcadia was lavishly equipped with mill houses—residences where workers boarded, usually without choice, either as part of their compensation or for a fee deducted from wages.

The print works in Arcadia had a large facility.

The print works offices are on the right.

The Barber store served shoppers in Arcadia.

Kenyon Mill in Kenyon descends from a saw-milling and iron-working operation in place by 1772.

THE MILL, KENYON, R. I.

27817

Kenyon Mill, now Kenyon Industries, for many years was home to Kenyon Piece Dyeworks.

74

The Langworthy Machine Shop fire, on the Hopkinton side of Wood River, was clearly a disaster. It would have been far worse but for a new steam pump supplying hoses from the Mystic Mill, facing Langworthy on the Richmond side, just left of this photograph. The stone Hope Valley dam here probably dates to the mid-1700s, well before the Revolution.

The Charmichael Mill Building, once home of Columbia Narrows Fabrics, for years was a landmark of Shannock.

The drying room at Richmond Lace Works (now Charbert's) in Alton was necessarily extensive.

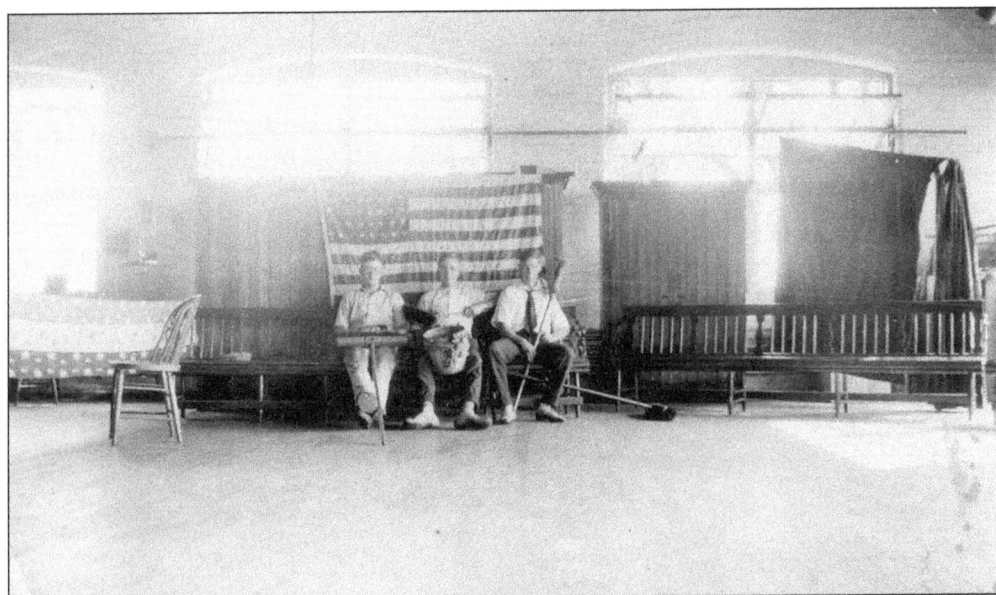

Workers held dances in the drying room. These fellows seem eager to get started.

An overhead conveyance moved lace from one building to another. These arrangements could be elaborate. One ran from the upper mill in Wyoming to the lower mill at the Route 3 bridge.

Mrs. Arthur K. Collins was "floor lady" to this group of finishing room workers at the lace works.

It will take them quite a few hours to get through those bundles!

There is nothing like a ukulele to liven up a long day working lace. Notice that the automobile's steering column is on the right side.

Baseball or softball livened up breaks at Richmond Lace Works.

Even if mills by the 20th century used steam or electric power, they still lay along their historic streams. Richmond Lace workers could get in a swim now and then.

Carolina, like most communities, had its own telephone exchange.

Richmond and Hopkinton both did much lumbering in the days gone by. This Wyoming basket shop no doubt took advantage of that work.

Chester (and later Nelson) Sherman maintained a clothing store on the square in Hope Valley for decades. Sherman's stamps (also issued by Hope Valley Hardware) rewarded loyal customers. The one-story brick block, originally erected by the elder Sherman, was razed in 2006.

Four

HIGH WAYS

The war is won, the Depression is finished, and times are good again! This young couple looks to the future with enthusiasm and confidence. Their car, and the freedom it gives them, are symbols of America in the baby boom. (Courtesy of HBH.)

The New Haven Railroad stopped in Shannock (seen here) and Kenyon. Now the nearest passenger stops (on Amtrak) are at Westerly and West Kingston.

Blasting out huge billows and piercing whistles, this steam engine raged its way through the cut in Shannock.

The train also stopped at this depot in Wood River Junction, so called because the stop was also the southern terminus for the Wood River Branch Railroad (WRBRR).

A gleaming 4-0-4 wood-burning steamer, with its nicely-detailed tender, served the line in its early days.

That steamer, or one very like it, adorned these 1877 stock certificates. The postage stamp served as a sort of seal to official documents. (Courtesy of LPL.)

On June 15, 1921, someone rode the whole line between Wood River Junction (in Richmond) and Hope Valley (in Hopkinton). Notice the X-shaped punch; conductors typically each had their own pattern. (Courtesy of LPL.)

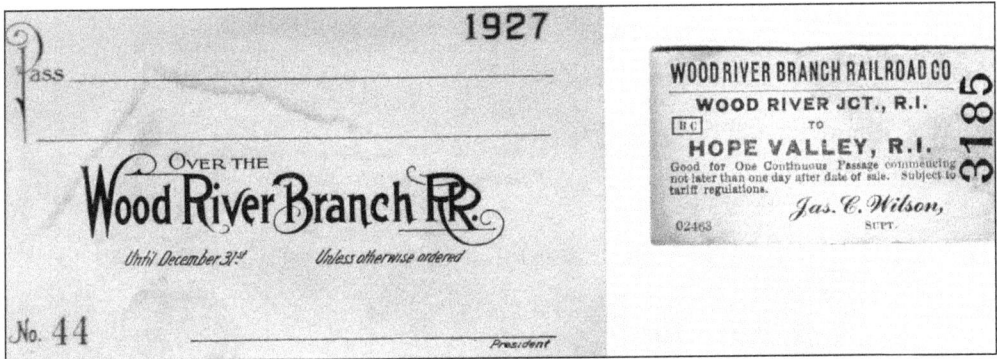

WOOD RIVER BRANCH RAILROAD CO
WOOD RIVER JCT., R.I.
B C   TO
HOPE VALLEY, R.I.
Good for One Continuous Passage commencing
not later than one day after date of sale. Subject to
tariff regulations.
Jas. C. Wilson,
02463   SUPT.
3185

Passes, of course, were highly coveted. (Courtesy of LPL.)

This gasoline engine was on strength in 1938. The WRBRR ran various locomotives in its career. (Courtesy of LPL.)

Unfortunately this streamliner was not a WRBRR engine! WRBRR officials are meeting the New Haven Railroad at Wood River Junction. (Courtesy of LPL.)

This is not a WRBRR passenger train, but a track car consist for inspections and maintenance, or for entertaining friends. (Courtesy of LPL.)

The Woodville passenger station (at the town line) may not have been especially aesthetic, but if one wanted a train, the WRBRR was the only game in town. (Courtesy of LPL.)

This 1917 Interstate Commerce Commission valuation appraised the station's contents at $223.10, the five-by-six-by-nine-foot outhouse at $81 even. (Courtesy of LPL.)

Dawley Tavern was a favored stop on the New London Turnpike, where Route 138 leaves Route 3 in Wyoming. Some of these rigs are doubtless here for pickups at the C. C. Perry General Store on the street level, perhaps loading the bone and phosphate advertised at the near end of the porch roof. A photographer has his studio a little farther down the front. There is also a coopery and a variety store.

Dawley Tavern is now the Stagecoach House. (Author's collection.)

In the early days of motorcars, someone lost control on the bridge at Alton. Is that a picnic basket on the bridge, or a tool basket?

A photographer was quickly on the spot, snapping shots and hurrying postcards onto the market. Look at the derrick that workers have erected to hoist the vehicle, which has now lost its fabric top.

This operation gives a nice view of how simple the early automobile could be, with a chain drive, small engine, and steering column on the right.

The photographer doubtless intended to give a view of Alton, but has also preserved the state of roads around 1900—dirt or mud, and rutted by narrow wheels.

The Jolly Miller combination garage and tea room in Hope Valley (around 1920) seems ready to meet the motoring public's every need, from tires to oil, air, gas, ice cream, tobacco products, novelties, stationery, periodicals, and even dancing, not to mention tea. This later became the site of Barber's grocery. The old Hope Valley School (attended by many Richmonders) is just visible behind the martin house. The home at left is still in use.

This coupe reminds one of the early automobile's design origin in the carriage industry.

Until the roads got paved, getting around by automobile could be an adventure. Kenyon Road, on the east side of Wood River Cemetery, looks like it is too deep under water to make this trip worthwhile.

The line of the west side of the cemetery at Wood River Church marked the eastern bound of the Shannock Purchase in 1709.

During World War II, even the humble bicycle promoted patriotism. (Courtesy of DAH.)

Five

SCHOOL DAYS

Hilda Florence Hoxsie posed
for a memorable photograph
when she was graduated, at
age 13, from Carolina School.
The year was 1916. Richmond
had 16 local school districts
before consolidation in the
20th century.

Carolina had a fine facility, later superseded by the Richmond School. Carolina School is now a private home.

Carolina seventh and eighth graders, along with their teachers, turned out for a photograph in 1932. The boys' high stockings are elegant—maybe that style should come back.

The 1933 class at Carolina seems a little uncertain about the future, or at least about the camera. George Conlon (standing third from left) seems a little worried by all the attention he is getting.

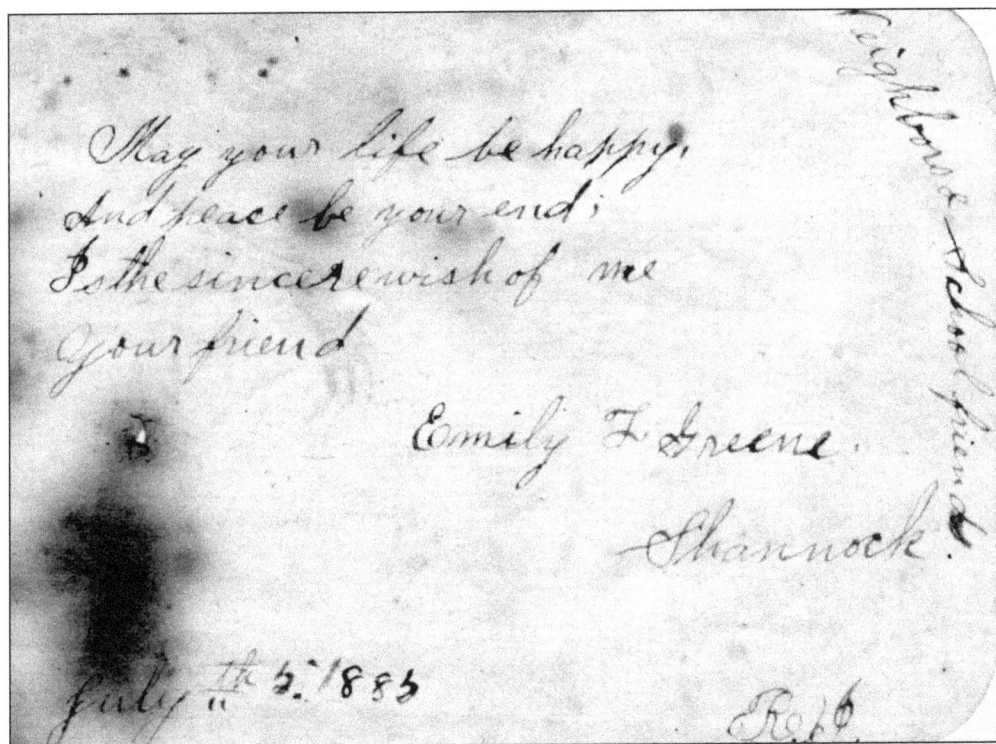

This 1885 note betokened the affection of a pair of Shannock friends.

Shannock's later Pawcatuck Grammar School had a fine, large facility, and a commanding place in the community.

Quarrelsome Corners School (District 5) stood near what is now Route 112, at the intersection of Kenyon Hill Road with Wilbur Hill Trail.

Bell School (District 9, here pictured in 1898) actually preceded and was absorbed into the formal town system. While the Bell School stood at the north end of Hillsdale Road, students were mostly drawn from the Tug Hollow neighborhood.

Florence Richmond, a beloved long-term teacher at Bell School, revisited around 1960.

Teacher Emma Palmer took this photograph of her school in 1924. Notice that a "porthole" has replaced the double windows above the door.

Isabelle Frazer MacLennan, who taught at Bell School from 1929 through its closing in 1934, gleefully bought herself a new car as soon as she got the job.

These 1915 picnickers at the Bell School from left to right include teacher Estelle Kenyon Sheldon, Elsie Kenyon Sheldon, Leonard Clark Sheldon, and John C. Sheldon.

All the Bell School students in this 1932 photograph are either Whitfords or McElroys.

Some of the Bell students (and a few who may be a little past school age) gathered for this photograph in 1933.

Even considering that school clothes were more formal back then, this group of friends is probably gathered on some special occasion.

Certificate of Attendance.

This is to Certify that _M. Olive Gardiner_ has attended the _Bell_ School in the Town of Richmond, Rhode Island, every day during the Term ending _March 15_ 190_7_.

_____ Teacher.

Chas. Greene,   Superintendent of Schools.

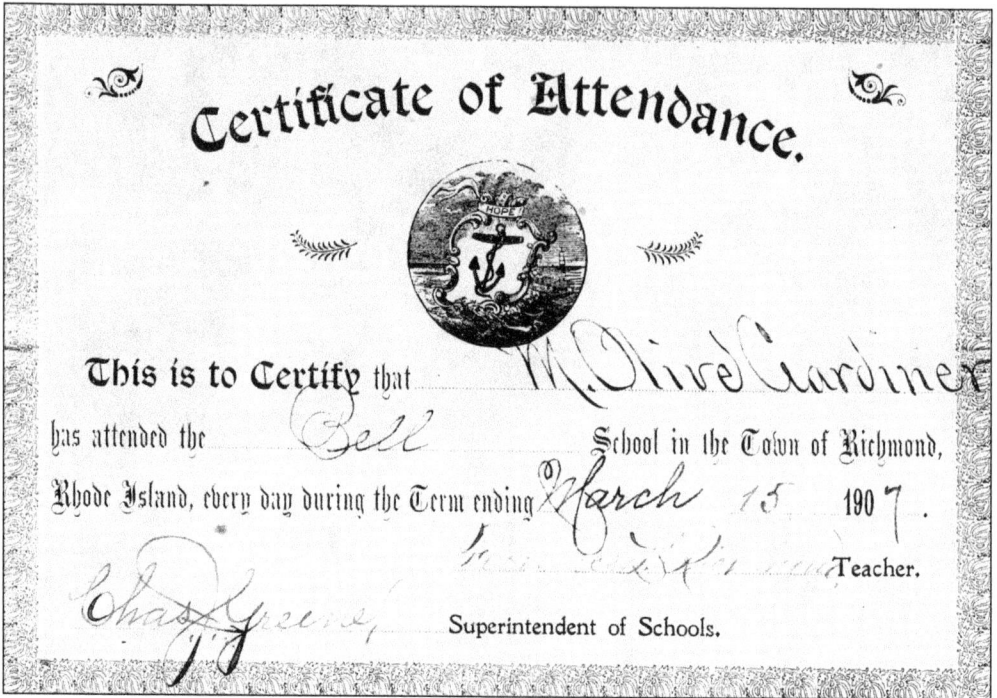

Olive Gardiner Kay saved her attendance certificates from the Bell School.

SIMPLIFIED SCHOOL RECORD SYSTEM

Bell School

Report of _Byron Smith_   Grade _8_

E, excellent; G, good; F, fair; U, unsatisfactory; VP, very poor.

YEAR	Half Days Absent	Times Tardy	Times Dismissed	Conduct	Reading and Literature	Penmanship	Arithmetic	Spelling	Music	Drawing	Manual Training	Domestic Arts	Physiology and Hygiene	Language and Composition	Grammar	Geography	History	Civil Government	Probability of Promotion
1928 to 1929																			
1st Quarter	4	0	0	E	G	G	G	E	G	E	E		E	G	G	E	E		
2nd Quarter	12	1	0	E	E	G	E	E	G	E	E		E	G	E	E	E		
3rd Quarter	15	1	0	E	E	E	E	E	G	E	E		E	G	E	E	E		
4th Quarter		2	0	E	E	E	E	E	F	E	E		E	G	E	E	E		

Below Signature of Parent or Guardian

1st Quarter		3rd Quarter	
2nd Quarter		4th Quarter	

Form 105   FILING EQUIPMENT BUREAU

Byron "Beanie" Smith had a good report in 1928–1929.

108

Phoebe Richmond taught school in Alton, after cycling from Arcadia to Hope Valley, taking the train to Wood River Junction, and walking the rest of the way.

Arcadia School (District 13) shows the pump without which no one-room school would be complete, along with the stone walls and scrub pines without which no picture of Richmond and its sister towns would be complete. Some schools maintained separate doors for boys and girls. Maybe Arcadia did the same.

The Arcadia girls seated third and fourth from left wear matching dress materials; the girls seated sixth through eighth have their own match. Presumably each group represents a set of sisters. Notice the boots or high-topped shoes that nearly everyone is wearing. The teacher stands fifth from left.

Hillsdale School (seen here around 1915) stood near the Punchbowl Trail. The stone slab in front of the door now lies at the door of Bell School house, in its new location by Richmond Town House.

In 1934, Richmond consolidated its schools into a distinguished 1–9 facility across from the town house. With aesthetically-compatible additions, it now serves as one of four elementary schools in the Chariho (Charlestown, Richmond, Hopkinton) regional system.

Richmond School's 1935 baseball team looks ready for all comers.

Hazel Travers (left) and Lois Murtagh Brophy joined an unidentified Richmond School staff member for this windswept photograph in April 1942.

A 1948 proposed Richmond high school would have comported perfectly with the architecture of the elementary school, but the project never came to pass.

In the early 1950s, Richmond School eliminated its ninth-grade program, graduating its students after grade eight. Students wanting to go to high school elected to attend in Westerly or South Kingstown, with Richmond taxpayers picking up the bill.

Bell School, which was moved to the town house grounds in 1971, is pictured here in 2006. Richmond School is in the background. (Author's collection.)

Bell School is once again a place of learning. These upper elementary students visited in 1985. Eleanor Smith stands in the doorway.

In 1959, contractors began clearing ground in Richmond for the new Chariho Regional Junior-Senior High School, which would serve 7th through 12th graders from Charlestown, Richmond, and Hopkinton. At the time, each town continued its own kindergarten-through-sixth-grade schooling; the regional district now covers kindergarten through 12th grade.

Earl Smith, a graduate of the Bell School and former town councilman, was one of many Richmonders who took a close interest in Chariho's progress. Notice the light-on-dark license plate, then used in alternate years.

Soon the gym and other areas took shape in the fields near Wood River Junction.

Ella Reynolds joined Cynthia Payne, Amey Reynolds Payne, George Payne, and Earl Smith on an exploration of the rising facility. Cynthia Payne, after attending Richmond School, became an alumna of Chariho and later a Chariho teacher. Richmond has many such links between its past and its future.

Six

CHILDREN'S HOUR

Potatoes, corn, or turf? This young baby boomer looks all set to carry on Richmond's traditional occupation. (Author's collection.)

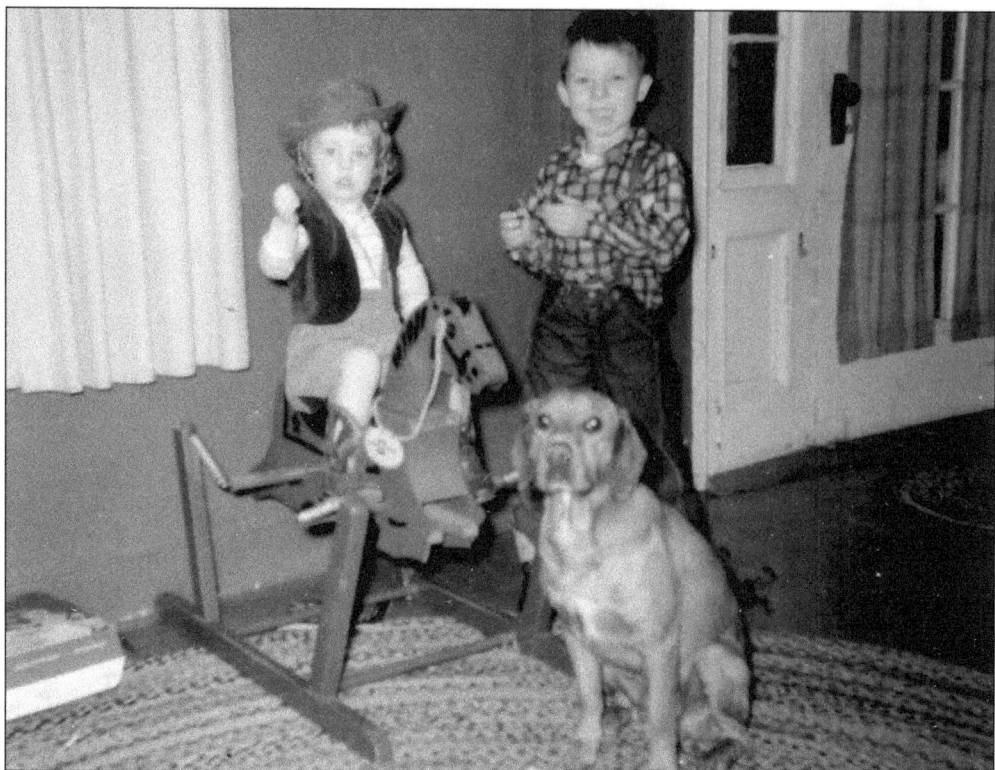
Kids, a dog, and a cowgirl suit—what a perfect picture of America in the 1950s. (Courtesy of HBH.)

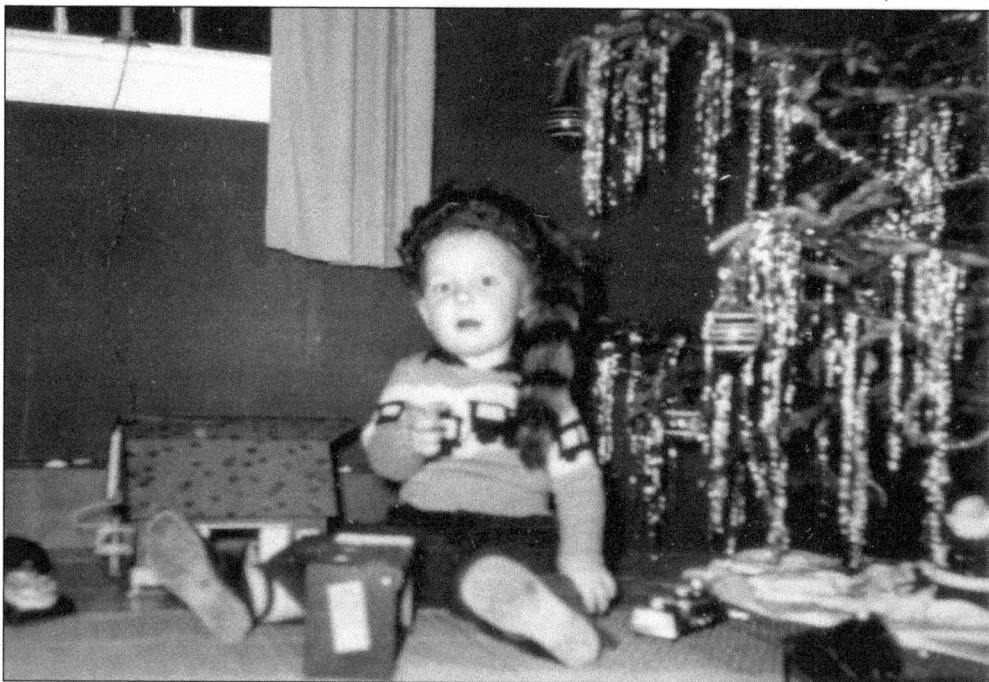
Likewise, the electric train, the rotary toy telephone, and especially the Davy Crockett coonskin cap infallibly evoke the time. (Courtesy of HBH.)

The western theme was also popular earlier in the century. (Courtesy of HBH.)

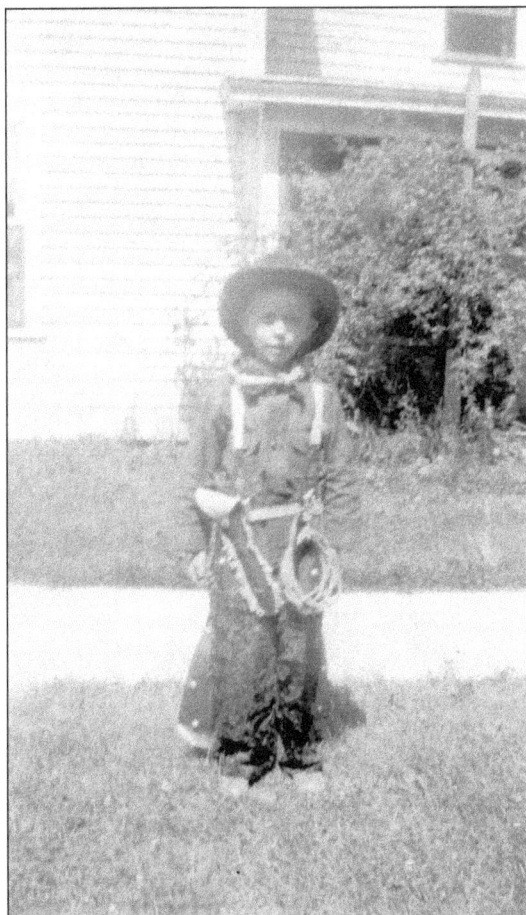

Nelson Sherman tried the cowboy look in the 1920s. (Courtesy of DAH.)

Curiously, Nelson Sherman is the only one with a lollipop. (Courtesy of DAH.)

Here Sherman tries his hand at golf. On the left is probably Dorothy Worden. In the center are Dot Fecteau (in rear) and Janice Dow.

Chester Sherman's straw boater and bow tie are signs of another age, but the tent could be found in the back yard today. Lula Kenyon Sherman stands with her children, Nelson and Barbara. The garage still stands on Main Street in Wyoming, now converted to a real estate office. (Courtesy of DAH.)

The Sherman home in Wyoming included a lovely fish pond. (Courtesy of HBH.)

Apart from the footgear, this Halloween crowd could take to the 21st-century streets, although they look a little unenthusiastic. (Courtesy of DAH.)

Everyone appears well bundled-up for the New England winter. (Courtesy of HBH.)

Cliff Pepler, on the left, may want a front tooth for Christmas, but good sledding weather will keep him occupied until then. (Courtesy of HBH.)

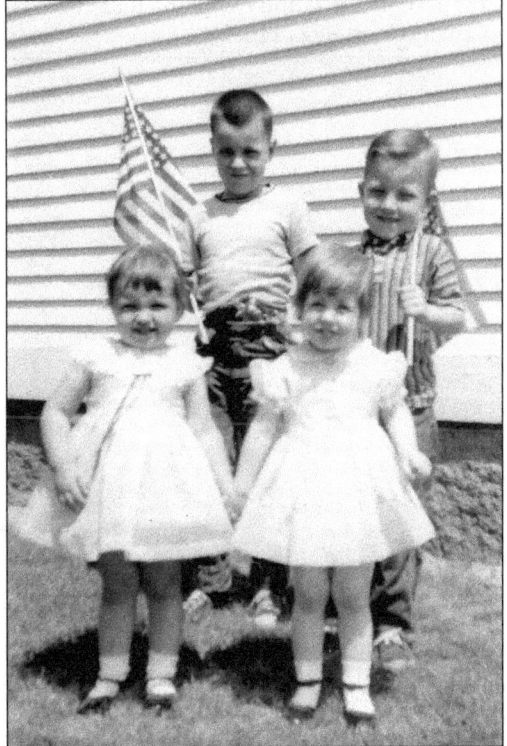

Judging from the summer styles and the flags, this could be the Fourth of July. (Courtesy of HBH.)

Cousins Lori Baton and Deborah House were both born in Westerly Hospital on New Year's Day in 1955. (Courtesy of HBH.)

The girls' mothers (Carolyn and Janice Dow) celebrated Memorial Day in the 1930s. The parade ran from the Depot Square in Hope Valley (where it still begins) to Wood River Cemetery. Some disagreement seems to have just passed between Carolyn and the small boy. (Courtesy of DAH.)

The play *Rose Dream* required a large cast of children and a substantial wardrobe.

The Depression was still on in 1939, a murderous hurricane had struck the year before, a world war was only months away—but for an hour, at least, smiling faces held sway at the *Mother Goose* recital. One could do far worse than be a kid in Richmond.

www.ingramcontent.com/pod-product-compliance
Lightning Source LLC
Chambersburg PA
CBHW050544110426
42813CB00008B/2256